ABCs of Basketball

For Denzel and Ezekiel

ISBN 9798378884018

First edition.

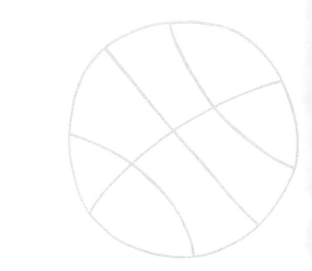

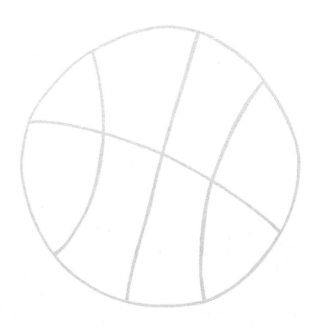

ABCs of
BASKETBALL

by Brittany Mack

MOOSE + GIRAFFE PUBLISHING, LLC

The team is here and they're ready to play, and they're going to teach you all about the game! They're so excited to have you as a trainee, and to show you basketball from A to Z.

Aa

A is for assist, when one teammate helps another score. Number 3 alley oop's the ball to number 11, and the team's points go up by two more.

Bb

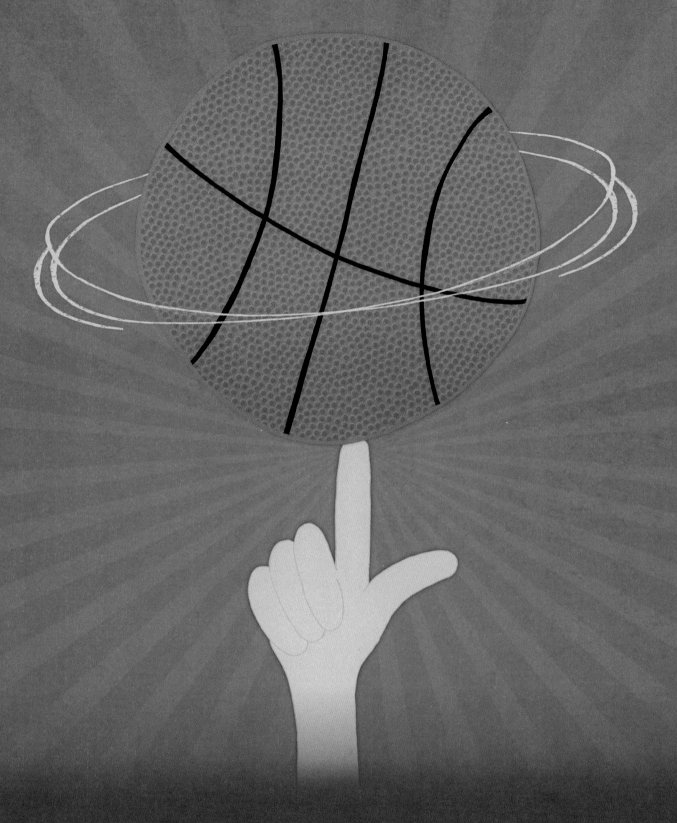

B is for basketball, it's what the team use to play the game. The players dribble, pass and shoot it, and no two players handle the ball the same.

Cc

C is for coach, he's the leader of the team. He teaches the players all sorts of things and helps them achieve their biggest dreams.

Dd

D is for dribble, players bouncing the ball up and down. Number 20 can dribble between his legs, behind his back and all around.

Ee

E is for effort and energy, what a player shows when he's giving his best. He works really hard during practice and games, then heads on home for some much needed rest.

Ff

F is for free throw, an extra shot one player gets to take. Number 15 adds a point to the team's score, all because the opponent made a foul mistake.

Gg

G is for guarding the opponent, working to keep him away from the basket. Number 20 is guarding his man so well that instead of shooting he has to pass it.

Hh

H is for the hoop that the team shoots the ball into. It comes with a backboard and a rim, and with a net that makes a fun 'swish' sound, too!

I is for inbound pass, made with only a few seconds on the clock. Number 15 must catch and quickly shoot it while being careful not to walk.

Jj

J is for jump, the players getting high up in the air. Number 31 jumps up to block a shot, and tips the ball to his teammate with care.

Kk

K is for key, and at the top is where the point guard might be. He dribbles the ball from behind the line and waits for his teammate to come off a screen.

L is for layup, an easy way to score. Number 11 tosses the ball up to the basket and it bounces in off of the backboard.

Mm

M is for man-to-man, when each team member guards a specific opposing player. Four minutes in and the opponent hasn't scored, as the team's defense silences all the naysayers.

Nn

N is for number, a player is known by the one he wears. The fans make signs to cheer for their favorite, and they hold them up everywhere.

Oo

O is for offense, when the team has the ball. Number 20 brings the ball up the court, and listens for his coach to make a call.

Pp

P is for practice, the team does it every day. They do dribbling drills and run and scrimmage to be ready for the next game they'll play.

Qq

Q is for quick, number 15 has such great speed! He runs and dribbles up the court and moves around with ease.

Rr

R is for referees, they do their jobs with care. They watch the players' every move to make sure they all play fair.

Ss

S is for steal, and number 31 causes a turnover. It's easy for him to get the ball when the opponent is running slower.

Tt

T is for team, five players on the court work together as one. They play the game really hard, but also like to have some fun!

Uu

U is for uniform; the jersey, shorts and shoes. Fans love it when they wear their throwback version, because the team never seems to lose!

Vv

V is for victory, and the home team comes out on top! They played such an exciting game that the fans didn't want it to stop.

Ww

W is for the water that the players like to drink. The hydration helps them focus on the game, so they don't have to over think.

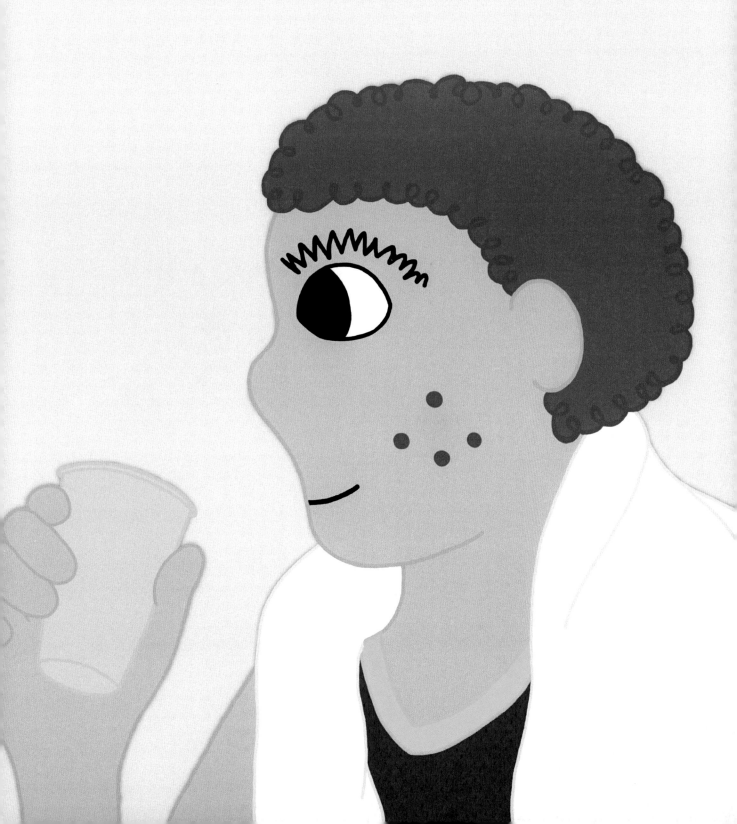

Xx

X is for x's and o's, coach uses them to draw up plays. There are five of each and a bunch of arrows that are all pointing different ways.

Yy

Zz

Z is for zone, a defense the opponent can't get past. The team works hard at it during practice, so during a game they can execute real fast.

Thank you for being such a great trainee!

A lot of fun was had while showing you basketball from A to Z.

GLOSSARY

OF

TERMS

Assist

A pass from one player to another that leads directly to a made basket.

Referenced on page A.

Alley Oop

A pass high above the rim that allows a player to catch and slam dunk or drop the ball into the hoop in one motion.

Referenced on page A.

Block (Blocked Shot)

When a defensive player makes contact with the basketball and prevents it from going into the hoop so that the opposing team does not score.

Referenced on page J.

Defense

The basketball team without the ball.
The act of preventing the opposing team from scoring.

Referenced on pages M, Z.

Dribble (Dribbling)

Bouncing the ball off the floor continuously with one hand. Players must continuously dribble while walking or running with the ball.

Referenced on pages B, D, P, Q.

Drills

Activities the players perform to improve their skills.

Referenced on page P.

Execute

To perform a task. (The team works on their zone defense during practice so that during a game they can get into the correct positions really quickly and play the zone defense.)

Referenced on page Z.

Free Throw

An unopposed attempt to score by shooting from behind the free throw line. The shooter may not cross the free throw line and opposing players are not allowed to try and block the shot.

Referenced on page F.

Foul

Illegal personal contact or unsportsmanlike conduct on the court or sidelines during a game. Most fouls involve contact that impedes on an opposing players' gameplay.
Referenced on page F.

Guard (Guarding)

When the defensive player positions his body between the opposing player and the basket in an effort to prevent the opponent from advancing the ball toward the basket or taking a shot.
Referenced on pages G, M.

Hydration

When the body is provided an adequate amount of liquid (water).
Referenced on page W.

Inbound Pass

A pass made from a player who is standing out of bounds (outside of the court) to one of his teammates who is on the court. The player has five seconds to make the pass once he is handed the ball by the referee. Once the inbound pass is made, gameplay is resumed.
Referenced on page I.

Key

The area below and in front of the basket; the rectangle that extends from the baseline to the free throw line. The key is often painted a different color than the rest of the court and is also commonly called "the paint" or "the lane."
Referenced on page K.

Layup

A two-point shot attempt made by leaping from below the basket and using one hand to bounce the ball off the backboard and into the basket. When doing a layup, the player lifts the outside foot (the foot away from the basket). The layup is considered the most basic shot in basketball.
Referenced on page L.

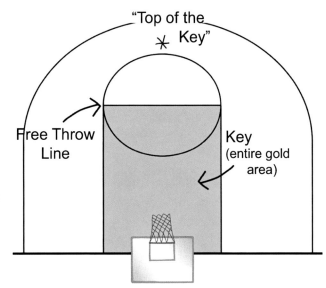

Offense
The basketball team that has the ball.
A team's method to score baskets and get open shots against the opponent.
Referenced on page O.

Screen
When one player stands beside or behind a defender so that his teammate can move around the defender and get open to receive a pass or take a shot. The defender is prevented from following and guarding his opponent because the player setting the screen is in his way. A screen is also commonly called a "pick."
Referenced on page K.

Scrimmage
An unofficial (practice) game. Scrimmages are often played during practices and involve players on the same team competing against each other.
Referenced on page P.

Steal
When a player forces a turnover by taking the basketball from the opponent or deflecting a pass.
Referenced on page S.

Turnover
When a player loses posession of the ball before taking a shot, and the opposing team gains posession of the ball.
Referenced on page S.

Walk
A dribbiling violation that occurs when the player with the ball moves without dribbling. Walking is also commonly called "traveling."
Referenced on page I.

Zone
A defensive strategy in which defenders guard specific areas of the court instead of opposing players.
Referenced on page Z.

Acknowledgements

Special thanks to Ovid, the ideator behind this book.

Thanks to Denzel and Ezekiel for being our testers, and for helping color the images.

Additional thanks to Cierra and David for their input on the text and images.

About Moose + Giraffe Publishing

Moose + Giraffe Publishing, LLC was founded in 2021 with the idea of creating children's books that teach educational fundamentals, such as ABCs, colors and counting, through the context of a favorite sports team.

Current available titles include*:

ABCs of Basketball [Men's Version]
ABCs of Basketball [Women's Version]
Colors of Football
Counting with Baseball
Counting with Softball

*Not all titles may be available for purchase through a given sales outlet

Select titles are available in an officially licensed version with the following collegiate properties:

Marquette University
University of Michigan

and more to come!

MOOSE + GIRAFFE PUBLISHING, LLC

Made in the USA
Las Vegas, NV
15 December 2024

70d57f6c-6f2c-40ca-85f6-7ed1832af009R02